OUT LOUD

poems

OUT LOUD

poems

PETER B. HYLAND

The Sheep Meadow Press
Rhinebeck, New York

Designed and typeset by The Sheep Meadow Press
Distributed by The University Press of New England

All inquiries and permission requests should be addressed to the publisher:

The Sheep Meadow Press
PO Box 84
Rhinebeck, NY 12572

Library of Congress Cataloging-in-Publication Data

Hyland, Peter B.
  Out Loud : poems / Peter Hyland.
    pages cm
  ISBN 978-1-937679-24-8 (alk. paper)
  I. Title.
  PS3608.Y54O97 2013
  811'.6--dc23
                         2013011065

The world breaks everyone and afterward many are strong at the broken places.

—Ernest Hemingway,
A Farewell to Arms

Mission accomplished, pal.

—John Berryman,
The Dream Songs, "16"

For Missy & Miles

ACKNOWLEDGMENTS

Many thanks to the editors of the following journals for first publishing the poems listed below:

American Literary Review: "Opening," "Storms Are Formed Behind the Storm We Feel"

Conduit: "Passenger"

Ecotone: "Lines Toward an Illuminated Manuscript"

Green Mountains Review: "Holiday," "Report"

New England Review: "Octoroon"

New South: "An Apology," "The Natural World," "Seeing Is Believing"

Pebble Lake Review: "Elegy to the Idea of a Child"

Ploughshares: "Lake Charles"

"The Natural World" was reprinted online at *Verse Daily*

Several poems within this collection appeared in a limited-edition chapbook entitled *Elegy to the Idea of a Child* (The Trilobite Press, 2009)

CONTENTS

MASH NOTE

That no person shall be born, nor die—the world's law,
Complete & invisible. Death

Is the punishment for death.
The penalty for birth is life.
We all have our sentences.

A flaccid Mylar balloon half-floats
Between the cars stopped at a light
On 43rd, dragging its ribbon, heading anywhere.

Happy Birthday. Look what I just made for you,

An image of senility, of mortality,
A gesture of affection, as when a dog
Returns to his master with a mangled bird.

Come over here, & let's trespass together a little longer,
So that the flame in my skull
Pushes higher, & behind
The hills where we have never been

Plumes of smoke blossom, one
After the other,
& gather into a dark bouquet.

My mind is in a thin red dress, curled up barefoot
On the sofa, one strap peeled low off her shoulder,
Waiting for you to come home.

DEFERRED DONOR

From the M. D. Anderson Cancer Center, doctors mail a diagnosis:
Because of your history, you must not
Donate blood, blood components, body organs or other tissues

Here or at any other blood or tissue bank.

Some people can't give themselves away. Listen,

In the city where everything has already happened,
   I'm riding in a haggard blue Toyota
With Jared & Chad. We are drunk, & happy. We are going places.
Across the interstate, headlights pass like a string of
   incandescent pearls.
The car disappears. On a couch at Terry's,

We are listening to Nirvana, the night charged with our affection.
We darken a spoon with a Zippo flame; the same needle,

It is entering the rivers of our hearts:

This is how, one night in October, I learned to share with others.

Today again, I read the hospital's letter, which they sent
   me a week after
I'd been turned away, because I admit to my body's history,
   admit that I once filled my veins

With easy pleasure passed between me & a couple of friends.

And it doesn't even matter all tests agree
That all's well in the kingdom of blood, that disease took a turn
   around another corner,
Because our stories are always happening, somewhere,
   & are preserved
By those who read us & who can't help but anticipate the ending.

This is why, when we talk about literature, we use the present tense.

PASSENGER

A bus emerges as if set adrift, is filled with chalky light
That makes the solitude of the one man riding

Seem decent. The light itself is solitude
Encased in dingy metal & scratched-up glass,

Where the man engraves sparrows with a pocketknife,
So that they inhabit his reflection.

I will not ask you to imagine it. You would see
The wrong bus, the wrong man who would only be yourself

Or the lover that held you like you were perishable
& is gone, &, wrongly, you would make the light sad,

Heavy & stupid, as you believe yourself to be
In such a light, when you pass through an intersection in the bus

You are imagining & mistake yourself for what you are.

Failed Narrative with Movements for a Musical Box

A buffalo head fixed to a lacquered plaque
Hangs beneath the crown molding. The hunter has placed it there

To give it time to think about man's tireless ingenuity
Which for many thousands of years has gotten the better of

Creatures that have ventured to exist within a hundred miles
Of a campfire or grocery, & about why it must therefore
   suffer perpetual

Humiliation, stuck to a wood-paneled wall in suburban Texas.
But inside its hollow form the head only keeps a pristine stillness,

& the glass eyes pretend to contemplate the scene below
Where it is already night, & the oak door shuts & opens,

Opens & shuts, stupidly, like the mouth of a fish.
And everyone is having a good time, because the parents

Are out of town, & since they are young the guests
All still believe they are virtuous. Within this scene,
   a girl slips her finger

Through the belt loop of her longtime crush, & pulls him closer.
On his jacket, a seriffed M stitched onto the chest,

Various insignia—numerals, chevrons, eagles, stars—the sleeves
A gray leather, his name on the back in chenille large script.

Then someone turns the volume up, for the guitar solo.
Two boys walk out from the bathroom down the hall,

Weary with euphoria, looking as if they have returned home after
Traveling a great distance, one kicking under the sofa a bottle cap

Emblazoned with a cartoon hornet. Blacklight,
Fantastic exhalations deepen the air, the room saturated

With an erotic thrumming, until the whole party begins to stare
My way, perks its collective ears, because I am there with them now,

At last the center of attention, the sudden host, balancing
At their faces a shotgun muzzle, extending an invitation.

This is real. I hardly know myself. I am, as they say,
Fucked up. Before me the town's good sons & daughters

Marvel at my potential, while I scrape against the moment,
Turning sharper, sharper, until I am as fresh

As a scalpel in the surgeon's hand. So much will change,
These my friends, their particular bodies, the timbre of their
    voices, their names

Which I withhold, I covet. I aim at their faces.
What they must think, you can imagine. Though perhaps
    you conceive

That I shun the intimate, because my telling is off kilter,
& that I harbor coldness, as one would a fugitive inside a cellar.

But I am only pulling you closer to let you glimpse
My shame, a tender animal hidden here among the rows.

Consider how it damages its belly with a single claw, making
Illegible inscriptions. Reach out & it crawls into your palms.

You feel below the golden fur, finding its most delicate part, a key
Like those used to wind the music box

Within a teddy bear from childhood, the kind that played
Goodnight, Irene or *Für Elise*, where a hundred metal
   fingers stretch to feel

A hundred pins revolving on the cylinder
Beneath the stitching, playing in the way the blind read, touching

Each note. But twist the key, & shame starts clicking,
Stuttering. It hiccups like a baby, growing scared.

Shame breaks loose & falls among the grass, & you follow it
With the twin barrels of the retinas—chasing, sporting—

While it scurries through the linguistic tendrils & stems,
Between the kerning, down into the hole at the end of the sentence.

Around us the wilderness stirs. Fauna prepare
For the gloaming. Headless herds careen toward the sun,
   unremorseful.

Up the vanished trail, there is a room where I threaten,
Where no one gets hurt, where everyone almost escapes.
  Josh, Michelle,

High school rivals, girl with the silver bow, dope dealers, Sean
Who totaled his truck against a tree on Shiloh Road,

Chad dead from an overdose at age twenty-four,
Sad beautiful Sadie dancing drunk on a chair,

Jeremy, Carlos, Damon out on Lake Texoma, warmhearted Holly,
Gina, comrades, patriots, assholes,

Frank the maligner, the cowboy who crashed through
   our front gate,
Terry arrested for statutory, destroyed lovers,

Future farmers of America, ravers, flag twirlers, darlings
Don't leave. I am trying to tell you a story.

LOST FRIENDS

Our old lost friends they are somewhere past the railhead
      At town's edge
We feel their laughter thriving out to greet us now no matter
      Where love or work
Has taken us to the Northern Ridge to Lawton to San Francisco
      No matter they come back
Like flames conjured by the wind on fading coals & leave
      Like ash each time
They come you see them less you cannot describe them
      To your new friends
Over coffee cannot explain their faces years ago
      They are possibly alive
In the stockrooms of Lewisville department stores
      Heaving boxes or
On the gravel of backroads they are laying down wisdom
      To each other
As their bodies ache toward the vacancies of their futures they
      Are loud & coltish
& gathered at wooden tables relieved with their initials drinking
      Beers to their own
Simple health to the gorgeous purity of a few common hands
      As you left them
Though there is so much memory you cannot remember if you knew
      Anyone at all

Name-dropping

So there I was again with Sadness.
Our decapitated smiles floated across the gloss
Of the society pages we had spread
Between us in adoration.

A Woodford Reserve, neat, for my friend;
For me, polyurethane on the rocks,
Said Sadness to our server.
In a red vinyl booth,

Failure & Fame made guns
With their thumbs & forefingers,
Sending intangible slugs into their opposing chests,
Giggling like happy criminals.

When Love arrived, a paparazzo snapped
An image of her pouty vulva, denuded inside
Her hiked-up skirt, as she exited the limo.
And at once the colossal flat-screens clicked on

In three hundred million American brains,
Broadcasting the megapixels, & everyone tried to affix
To their mouths the expression
Love wore between her legs.

I know how this sounds. These days,
All the hip kids stand in contrapposto,
Clad in shades and dark leather,
Smoking ironies, extinguishing the butts

On the backs of their hands, until a perfect O burns
Through to the palms, & they hold an emptiness.
Being cool. Being scared.
Because the totemic certainties have now slumped

To the curb, & I am bewildered, in wonder,
Listening to the distant slender thrum of an engine driving
Toward me up the road, which may never arrive.
Did I mention that I also know Death?

LAKE CHARLES

A gas flare throbs, an ignition
Urged out from the interlacing steel.
Over the refinery, it hovers,
So long as pipelines rush raw oil
Thrilling through
A circulating need, so long
As a man must be propelled
Forward & his engine filled.
The burning occupies the black air
Like a moth transfixed—
Still living, fluttering, a golden blur.
It is extinguished & returns.
Faintly illuminated
By dashboard light, travelers
Pass & are compelled
At the speed by which they are driven.
They reach a familiar, temporary,
Carved-out space where a bed
Extends like a tongue to receive them,
& they dissolve
Into a fog of linens. Enthroned above,
The flame beats its wings & scatters
Heat on the city, on motels,
On the two-storied suburban squares
Where families sleep
& look with closed eyes toward it,
Sensing the thin imperceptible
Valves buried at their centers
That take & release what is given,
Currents washing out
& into the fleshy cylinders,
Stirred by the spinning cranks,
The dark secretions, the yearnful,
Hollow mechanism of the organic.

FIREWORKS ON LAKE TRAVIS

Swimmers waft their buoyed
            Skeletons over cooled
Greens of the lake's interior
                 Back to their hulls,
The ships powered
            With the moon's high glow

& lit within,
        A length of lanterns strung

           Together, tangled
Under stars,
        Of which they are a sort of mimicry.
Straining up the side ladder,
                A boy bears a world
Heavier than the lake,
            But not more difficult,
Himself meaning only
             A different thing

        Above the waves or beneath them.
He stands wet
           & stares at the hills;
Air cracks when the first goes up.
                  What he sees
Is not the scene reflected
In the boat-shattered lake.
                It is not the reds
That briefly glaze his body.
Not the sight
            His own eyes throw out
        To the bursting flame,

That is not a star.

SUBEROTIC

On channel 151, a schizophrenic blizzard,
Glimpse of an arm as it reaches for something urgent
Before being subsumed into an electric whorl.

The cable company is scrambling
What we shouldn't see, what we haven't paid for.
My cousin & I wait for the next naked fragment to surface

Or talk to slip through the distortions surging the frequency.
Tit, cock. Words we don't know we're learning,
So easy to say. Silly, but serious,

Like the toy with removable cartoon parts—
Fat plastic eyes, pink ears, a grin white & swollen.
Open the back & let the pieces tumble.

Arrange them to make a face, a body,
Which comes apart again like nothing. Fun,
But very serious. We are still young enough

To fit under my parents' bed.
My cousin, her dark hair. I don't know I shouldn't want
To touch it. That I want to touch it.

When we look up at the screen, a woman steps forward,
Head & arms lost in static—
Nike of Samothrace, winged Victory,

A statue made more beautiful by what it lacks,
Which the ancients would have called broken.
She unravels, a million acidic

Threads twist into the visual buzz.
Cousin. Woman. Victory. Her.
Our limbs are pure white marble, tossed

In sacred alleys. In strange meadows.
Beneath the beds of our fitful parents,
Who stroke each other with a kind of revulsion.

OF BODIES CHANGED

—OVID

When they come poolside
& lay out, arms spread & folded back
To let the chest unfurl,
Luxuriant with heat,
Or as they shimmer
Their own good-looks uncontrollably
At the deep end,

I can see why Naiads
Would churn for youths
Who bathed in their silvery waters,
& for a moment I am with them,
Leering from the undergrowth.

The old gods knew a body
Is a temple to be entered,
& in the sheer clamor of their divinity,
In whatever form their love required,
They chased mortals who sprung haunches
Or collapsed into a flower
Because beauty makes all things seem permissible.

And so my body wonders at the shape
It takes as I watch these few men swimming.
We are the same element: two stones
Struck together will make a fire.
What, if we touched beneath the shallows,
Would spark from us?

The sun may still be a god.
Let his burning eye
Find me lounging in this plastic chair,
The pool pump whirling
The chlorinated water, those bronze backs
Flashing & diving, my aspect changing...
Oh, that I were enough to bring him down!

Uncertainty

The consciousness of a sparrow,
Sensation at birth of the initial air, of exteriority,
Money without the resentment
In having or not having it,

All who I've eased or hurt through living:
Most things I'll never get to know. This even,
Why one Halloween I had my first kiss
With the Wicked Witch of the West,

Holed up in a basement closet.
From the dark, our childmouths stretched
Toward the upland of our coming lives,
Like fawns accepting their eager legs

& rising to another world.
We smeared our make-up into each other
As the floorboards creaked with the party above,
Both of us a guide to our own becoming.

When I think back on thresholds I've endured,
The high & low, the insatiable horizons,
An unbinding whiteness disturbs my everyday heart.
How have I come this way?

AN APOLOGY

A woman's dress knows more than I do
About propriety. All day long it's over all the parts
That make an ache fly up me
Like pigeons shocked out of their sidewalk meals.

But leaning over a book, breasts will float
Like two thoughts pressed together, twin axioms
In a pure philosophy, the blouse barely
Regarding the genius that fills it.

Or a skirt sways open, is insouciant,
As if some miracles weren't abiding within,
As if it were a rug or tablecloth
Covering what nobody thinks of.

Underneath thrive the deepset cores, subcutaneous wells,
The pulp, the rubies buried beneath the rind.
I want to throw my eyes down
The pelvic slope, bare thigh, any of the thousand

Declivities that form the woman
Sitting right there in front of me.
A dress would never feel that way,
& I get sorry because my gaze is long, or not right.

But a tree, because it is, grows leaves & lets them drop,
Swells with fruit whether or not it wants to;
A woman in heels & a snug top is an orchard
Heavy with loveliness.

Each dress should wave like an ecstatic flag
Whenever a woman slips it on,
Should tear itself from her, dance down
The boulevard, & burst into conflagration

In a terrible display of tact.
Here this woman, or that one, I can't help
But mind her manners—
The eye keeps its own etiquette.

TEASE

Today I approximate the graces of a full grown girl.
I strut from shower to sink in my terry cloth skirt,
Flaunt my hips, just so.

Steam veils the mirror in sheets of white French silk tulle.
Someone on the other side is hankering
For a show, wishing the curtains would part.
I have him wait. I curve
My wrist & pivot on a heel.
I glance behind my shoulder like an odalisque,
Trying to make my face sweet,
A canvas-worthy muse.

All the rare ladies begin to titter inside Jansen's *History of Art.*
The Venus de Milo puts forth a groan.

Exhausted mistresses, poised within
Cold galleries, bare-breasted, bored
By the fondling of curators,
Your crotches shielded with one delicate hand,
Can't a man be flirty, a minx, if only once,
In the privacy of his own home?

Years back, when I asked a friend to pose for me, clothed,
It all came off anyway, & she selected postures
She had seen while skimming
A catalogue raisonné on Balthus,

Where bare schoolgirls lounged with a leg
Hanging off the sofa, enthralled by their own pubescence,
Dallying in the soft strange light.

With my pencil I sketched her shapes—the pale belly's curve,
Architecture of the bent knee, labial complexities,
Whatever I wanted
Page after page in my drawing tablet.
It was a way of having her.

Objects of desire! *Objets d'art*!
I let my towel fall, raise my fingers to the steam, & rip
A hole for my admirer. We face each other
For a long time. Our lips touch the glass.

NAMING

In Mali, the Bamana believe
That when a man speaks, his words

Are substance. His prayers cling,
Thickening over the altar.

Water he says & the word falls into the river.
At night the moon, large & impossible, rises.

He says *Please* & what he says
Coils into the air. Here, among those

With whom I am obscure, to whom
I am familiar, my enemies, my gods, I've said

So many things I haven't meant.
Too often my tongue has fluttered like a rag

In a ruthless wind: a threat, a joke, or a curse,
Which is how you praise the thing you hate.

I have named my tribes & have named
Them wrong. What do I know about people anyway?

Where does the language go? Somewhere inside,
A voice beats its head against

The walls that fill me. Friends, lend me
Your ears. I want to make you one word

That tears from my mouth like
Wings from a chrysalis.

PASTORAL SARTORIAL

You know, I'm the sort of person who can coast up
Interstate 5 through the Chuckanuts toward Bellingham
As the mist lumbers mutely between the peaks,

Some white birds shiftless in a field where
A thin rain lacquers a battered harvester,
& still I think only of the worsted wool

Ludlow suit (pg. 4, the J. Crew catalogue).
What's new this season? *Sublimity.*
The young dapper gentleman placed

In white suede bucks grins like an errant monk.
Trim silhouette, a modern cut.
The same countenance the conifers

Repeat past the road's reflective stripes unreeling
From a point so far off nobody ever
Bothers to travel there. The sky is gray linen.

Mountain deer slough their hides when footfall ruffles
The climate, & now all the bachelors have
Nice shoes to wear to happy hour.

Notice how to fashion one thing you must disrobe
Another. Or become disrobed. My mother was the garment
I let fall as I stepped to one day

Speed by this 4-door sedan blinking its hazards on the shoulder,
The bay close but hidden,
A thread of contrail reiterated on its water.

A wave's slow thrust. The wet murmuring of the wheels
On asphalt. The attic creaks in the cottage.
A voice calls for me using someone else's name.

But I can't hear any of it. Soon a strange
Hand will begin to finesse the invisible button
Of my bare neck & undo my placket down to my stomach.

When I slip from my body, I'll be like the puddle
That exposes itself to the sun
In the after-rain & becomes nothing.

STORMS ARE FORMED BEHIND THE STORM WE FEEL

—MELVILLE

Because no one in my life has been escorted,
Suddenly, around a dark corner,

& my jaw has never wilted beneath a soldier's heel
Or hunger twisted in me like a mob of snakes, a living knot,

I suppose I am denied a certain wisdom.
When terror lisps into my ear,

What should I yell out at the night, where my neighbors deliberate
Their way through a twelve-pack

While the patio exudes a citronella sweetness?
I breathe it in, walk just out of view,

& piss beside the lantana that I've let
Grow headhigh. I kiss an umbel.

Tomorrow I'll take the shears to it, because it obscures
The hose & spigot, which is to say

For no good reason. Such as others
Might treat me & those I love

If it suited them—barbarity & chance, maybe soon.
Stained trousers. Birds in the attic. Telemarketers dialing
    from wherever,

Interrupting dinner. Banal misfortunes,
Are these any kind of preparation?

The wind moves & the leaves start to sizzle.
First, the rain tossed loosely. Then, the squall.

My neighbors retreat into dull lamped interiors.
The storm purples like a fresh bruise.

It doesn't mean to be Nature's icon or the breath of an angry god.
It means only what I ask it to.

I'm going to stay here a little while at my open door,
Giving the weather some room to barge in & wipe its feet

On my floor & furniture. Quick white brilliance,
Followed by thunder.

Red florets shaking. Water pouring on metal. The blue of midnight,
& further back, a different blue.

OCTOROON

What the garden keeps will not wither,
But the garden keeps nothing. My grandfather
Built an arbor, upon which he trained

Vines of karaila, *momordica charantia*, the bitter melon.
During an afternoon one summer,
Michael & I are talking.

The gourds have almost ripened, a clutching
Meandering growth: muscular, fulsome.
We can see it from the window.

The daylight looks both very hot & very cold.
They're all the same... Michael says. The moment
Shifts, as if now anything can be spoken.

From a vine my grandfather pulls
A single harvest, the gnarled ridiculous fruit,
A warty phallus, the last thing you would think to eat

If asked to pick from the garden, its bitterness
A kind of delicacy.
They're all the same, those people.

He means the man who had touched
His sister, now pregnant.
He means my grandfather, kneeling at the greenery.

He means black people. Those people. He feels safe
Saying this, because I don't look like
Those people. I pass

For the upright white American.
I pass so near to you & yet you hardly know.
A wasp jabs itself into a pane of glass,

More than once, feigning impatience.
The garden breathes slowly.
A breath for summer, a breath for winter.

It keeps nothing—
My grandfather exhaled into a nimbus,
The arbor thinned to a vapor.

We are watching the mist tumble over
The leaves and make them brittle.
You continue to say terrible things,

So that I will pay attention
To the wasp fashioning an instrument, an organ
From mud, from what has been withered

& varied & gathered & built
Back up again, a nest of pipes
That vibrate with emptiness as the young rupture

The seals, their stingers
Adorned with beads of venom, this bitterness—
They do not want to hurt you, but will.

PARLOR GAMES

Everyone wanted a game,
So I brought out the puzzle-box.

Dark wood inlaid with a bright circled star,
Our friends passed it round, tinkering,
Learning its movable parts,

Searching its seams for a way in. Soon

They left. Later in bed, we both fretted
Trying to solve each other.

We turned as red as children
In their little fits, furious at the nerve
Of whatever is placed beyond, or above,

Or within them—human frailty or a cookie jar.

We mulled ourselves over, & then we
Almost set the pieces right,
But when one space fell

Open another closed, which is always
The case. And why we continue.

Unlike our friends, who failed at stubbornness.

Impossible they said to the box & preferred
Moving on to other problems
Traveling between us, each giving up.

So I showed them its trick, a thing
So simple no one thought to do it.

RECEPTION

There are rooms where lamps burn
Their thin filaments
To cast odd light across the faces gathered.

They are filled with some good friends who wander
The brie & Carr's,
Who polish off the last bottle of cabernet.

And you must always try to conjure up
Whose name it is that comes drifting forward
Amid the jeans & blazers

& fawning shoulders,
Or work to care about John's
Limp luck with that Russian girl

Or how gloss-lipped Jane finally
Got fucked by our suave Economy. Laughter
Fills the doorways.

A cold wind presses against the windowpane.
Each hand you touch
Is one touch closer to its end.

Loneliness arrives like a dark guest
Dressed for the occasion,
& you ask it in.

REPORT

Passion is an ill-favored thing, so you say my dear, sweet Plato.
On the television the politician arrives at a podium
To defend his offices: a city lost, some bodies found.

Acts of God, acts of Man, the same old stories.
Our tragedies are mostly typical, which is news to us,
The reworkings of our first hurts, variations on a theme we suffer.

And it all unmoves me,
Scenes of explosions with their crumpled adornments,
Rooftops like stones peering out from the water,

The dead beneath their makeshift shrouds, as if they were furniture
In an abandoned house, covered by a bedsheet
To keep the dust off—but it isn't overexposure.

I've just misplaced all tenderness somehow, & anger.
More than ever I want to be the type to burst
Each syllable & make a howl

For the used & unlucky, to have my goodness wild.
The women on an Athenian krater have torn at their heads
For a few millennia, & in the old poem

The soldier makes rage against one thing or another,
But I go on like the ruined crops, the ruined towns,
& the news only lasts an hour.

THE TORTURERS

He was sealed with a simple knot,
Except his mouth
Which was left
Unbound, so it could sing.

On his right side they tapped
A knuckle, & again
At each of his body's walls
They rapped, until the far end
Of the throat
Issued forth a little trill.

Soon others came, & each
Pressed an ear against him
& knocked,
So that they could tell
Where he was hollow.
It took months,

Years. He was not hollow.
But they liked
The sound it made:
The knuckles, the throat.

At last there was just
The song, which hung high above,
Like a tattered banner
In a public hall
Bearing the colors of the new
Republic.

JUNK MAIL

Today's deliverings all
Plead *Do Not Discard*. I toss
Them to the trash, a habit.

Pined for by bankers hurting
In Wilmington, who scroll down
Mailing lists as if they were

Counting loves, I recognize
What I've thrown out in others.
In myself more so. The bright

Irreplaceable gifts I've
Been given are gone, knocked out
In the heaped up past. Too bad,

Says my watch as it ticks off
Promises. Too bad, I say
When I break them every time.

HOLIDAY

Now is the season when small forests
      Appear in the supermarket parking lots
            So that families walk through

An afterlife of trees, choose one & promise it
      Some glamour, & hedges that line
            The lawns are gowned

In electric strands, whose bulbs pulse
      Or stay constant as the evening settles
            While the serene

Plastic figures huddle
      Beneath a collapsible manger, & we come home
            Holding too many

Bags in our hands, urgent & comic,
      Like two brimmed glasses teetering
            On top of a serving tray,

& the bells on our wreath shiver when I push in
      The door, & my wife turns on a lamp
            To find that someone has left us

A message—*I'm looking for my daughter.*
      If you are her...this is where
            She is listed. We'd like

To hear she's well... anything
   From her. Please call me. Her name is...
      But he forgets to leave

A number, & the Caller ID reads *Private*, & we turn happy
   Because we are saved from having
      To be decent people,

Who would dial up a stranger to acknowledge
   His gaping misery & say the right thing & worry a little
      On his behalf, but the tinsel

Is gleaming, & we are not his daughter, & his suffering
   Is distant & easy to erase, so we sing
      Along with Nat King Cole

O tidings of comfort... while we empty our bags,
   Glad we won't answer, that trouble
      Isn't spilled everywhere all over

The world, soaking into the fabric
   Of some new attire, the person wearing it
      Looking foolish, or worse.

Hard Times

You, there in the hard edges
Of an empty room—everything that belonged cleared out,

Given over to other spaces, other hands—
I want your cold gray floor of loss,

Those nailholes unplastered, that language of depressions
Written where the chairs once stood.

Lend me these hollows in the puzzle,
This presence of a thing removed.

I want what I'm not entitled to: grief whole,
Complete as the home I fill each day with my wide self,

Where I have many places to sit & contemplate
My three carved tables, & the paintings above,

& the delicate ceramics I return to after work's end,
All wholly undisturbed.

IDYLL OF THE RICH

A neighborhood parvenu has left
The bruised body of his Bentley dashed,
Tail first, into a run of fencing

That separates old greed from mounting greed.
On the green, the golfers are shouting.
The caddies are pointing.

Even a squirrel, smug in his branches,
Is seeming to disapprove:
Nobody likes the nouveaux riches.

And, although someone must surely call the police,
Although someone must polish this scene,
Nobody moves.

There is a bit of chenille tucked under a wheel.
Some pearls lie scattered across the manicured field,
White like teeth.

Something has happened irrevocably—
The Bentley has forfeited all repair.
The country club estimates its store of grief.

With care, the squirrel flits down through his mansion of limbs,
Down his one-columned manor,
Turns tail, & tends to the business of his estate.

OPENING

Following a small stir
Of grass, I knelt to earth
& caught a nimble grasshopper
In the mouth
I'd made of my hands.
He leapt there like an orgiastic tongue
Licking my palms
With his nervous shell.
Soon I brought him to the eaves
Where the garden spider
Set out her web,
& I cast him into
The end I'd spun him.
I watched
As he was kissed & dressed
Across the many netted threads
That trembled like delicate
Sinews of the universe.

I too am sometimes
Carried up by a fathomless will,
A clear broad strength I cannot
See the whole of.
I have found myself pitched against
Indeterminate walls:
I struggle as I struggle.
And so often have I been wrapped,
Cloaked in joys & losses,

I am under many layers,
Though a bright fang pierces me wherever
& my seams are torn.
At my inmost chamber, I shine,
I am molten.
Another life descends & enters.
I am opening.

SEEING IS BELIEVING

For my brother, gone to war

Of course, our father, but then also
Some unknown in my only oxford shirt,

Living frankly on the surface a reflection haunts,
Like he isn't me, which he's not. Some days

I'm startled by my mirrorself.
This morning, David, it is you as you were

When we lived off Westwood in college,
Where the lady next door, postmenopausal,

Mowed her patch of lawn in a two-piece display
Of stars & stripes, to the horror

Of us both, because everything needed to be young.
We shared with the waitress in the garage apartment

Our washer & dryer, & she'd leave
Her panties on the lid where we'd have to touch them

To start a new load or get an old one out,
& act like it was nothing

To hold the panties of a sexy girl.
Now, in another state, you nuzzle into your gun

As if it were your first darling, & your eyes purl
Behind your non-reflective goggles.

This is an old romance,
& someone's going to get a broken heart.

You need to break their hearts, come back
& never fall in love again. David,

More & more I look so unlike myself,
The resemblance is striking.

Lines Toward an Illuminated Manuscript

A boy has his hands full. The sky
Worries him, the sun pulsing, painful to look at.
As it is painful for the eye to rest
On a body which has been torn, where each wound
Is a mouth, & the mouths all make a red choir
To sing the body's suffering. He has
His hands full, so he nests in the shadow of a stone wall—
Almost patient, almost understanding himself.
What is he waiting for? Perhaps for someone to find him
Because he has learned his first truth,
That living is a form of loss, luxurious,
With its many textures: the sodden coats of lambs,
The knuckles of granite, the stalks & silks of the genitals...
But he is waiting for the men to come up the road.
Now they arrive. Their boots pull toward the earth
& the dust rises, clouding their ankles in yellow mist.
And the men are laughing, the way men laugh when they have labored
At a problem too difficult. Beyond human effort. Beyond cruelty
Or compassion. And having perfected their failure,
They grow content. If they were to see the boy,
See what he holds, their laughter would harden into a stone silence.
What is he waiting for? A few more paces, & soon
They will pass the row of date palms
& the shuttered market. Then their features
Will begin to distinguish themselves, their faces becoming particular.
So that he can say this man is not the other;
These men are not our own. And it is clear now.
The men wear helmets, whose colors resemble
The road, which itself resembles a cord pulled taut
Around the aching land. They raise their guns. Why is the boy
Before them? What has he thrown?

It drops to the sand like a fallen fruit. *Grenate,*
In the Old French. A pomegranate, as the goddess ate
To rule the dead. The berries bursting. The juice of them
Purpling the fingers. Dark seeds entering the flesh.
But he is still only learning, so the boy
Has forgotten to make the bomb ready—a child's mistake,
Innocent as the day is long—& at once it is in the soldier's palm
Who steps out, pulls the pin & gives it back. Blown
Into a rough calligraphy, the thick gold strokes
Of a brush dipped in ink that pools forever at the body's well,
The boy is translated into a thousand characters. The alphabet
Of misery & fortune. Of relentless grace.
And it is necessary, for boys
Will be boys, as our fathers have told us.
And men will go on aiming their trumpets of horror,
Playing a music that is ancient & regrettable.
And there are no enemies among us here where we gather
On a white field to build our struggles.
Are you necessary? Look what you hold in your hands.

At 3 A.M.

The rain has
A thousand
Hands that lull
My ears they lay
Themselves
Increasingly
Across the city
Smoothing
Out its folds I
Am one
More crease
Eased
Among the
Crumpled
World

ELEGY TO THE IDEA OF A CHILD

You transpired in an amniotic sea
Where the currents of your mother & me
Ran blindly together,
Blending our bodies' furtive elements
Which we can barely understand.
Godlike, you unlocked yourself
At the core of her belly & began to shape
Your distending world,
Outdoing the prescriptions we had inherited
To ward off your inconceivable becoming.
And through the ultrasound's grains,
The nurse peered into her interior,
Deciphering your cryptic anatomy:
The minuscule rhythms, the augury of your skeleton.
What we did not will we had undone.
I see your unknowable face sometimes buried
Beneath those of living children
Who came forth brilliantly
From their mothers' glad, convulsing wombs,
Learning the first motions permitted
To their airheavy lungs,
Their fathers looking on, moving to touch
The strange substance they had released
Painlessly from themselves,
Finding it now altered & returned.
I have generated a realm
In which to carry you where you haunt
Me through the energy that rises
As I look with or without care toward
Women who momentarily
Take me into their desire.
I do not know if I loved you;
Forgive me; I am not sorry.

Tough Love

Therefore I collected my small miseries into a red
      Duffel bag & like a real man
Told my mother I was gone that this was it
      & almost knocked the storm door
Off its hinges striding into our yard's slim wilderness
      Where I hid near the back wall

For hours I made a hot game of tears
      But lost finally picked up
My bag & headed back to the sun-dulled porch steps
      I shuffled to my bed in sobs
Watched darkness & heard the soft wet clinks
      As my mother washed the dishes

My father missed dinner off in his office tower
      Up under worn out clouds
Of east Manhattan I waited for the broad beams
      Of his '87 Mustang to search
Across my wall I waited into dream that night I sailed to him
      Bound off the Jersey shore

From my skiff I saw one gold fleck high in the city's skyline
      A solitary coin of light
I knew it had two sides one hidden one bright I traveled
      As waves beat my vessel forward
I woke confused my father's hands I thought
      Were those hard crests of ocean

As he stormed on me like a man who knew what it was
        To suffer weather his blear stare
Constant his briefcase in the corner both our elements
        Connecting somewhere inside
The calm wide eye of violence we entered
        Where we remain shadowed

So even now from down deep within the country
        Of my boyhood I hear him
Earnest with love my father walks through
        Our ineluctable house
Through doors leading inwardly passages
        I begin to know

THE NATURAL WORLD

One September the neighbor's terrier found a way
    To sneak through to the hens.
                He wrung each neck,

Scattering feathery mounds of white
    & red from the trough to the fence,
                An entire field of small

Mutilated pillows—
    That dog had never been happier.
                He trotted casually, surveying

The scope & pleasure of his
    Accomplishment. But I cannot accuse him
                Of being cruel. Poor puppy!

Morality is a trick no dog can learn.
    Because we feel guilt, some say we are better
                Off than the animals.

I agree, though I wonder at the dumb life
    Of a terrier, who is equally at his best as
                He sits shading himself

Beneath the ripening pears
    Or as he stops here & there, scampering along
                In a yard filled with broken

Chickens. When I doubt the soul, I see landscapes
      Cleared of all distinctions,
                Where no lines converge,

Where the fang that enters
      The human heart grows from a human mouth.
            The little beasts

Fulfill themselves over & over, & know
      No courts or fiery pits,
                Only the giving-in

To their great
      Doggy urges: chasing weakness,
              Running through the clover.

A VISION AT THE SHORE

The day was windless. Beside the calm dark pool, my face
Reflected off the surface. Grackles, each of their eyes

Like polished amber with a creature preserved
At the center, gruesome & extinct, spun wildly above,

Thousands, circling in the reflection, downward
Into the water. I thought this was an illusion. Then the pool

Began to eddy and distort my features. In my confusion,
I reached in to keep the image straight, but the water had

Its own skin, which I cut with my hands, & from the wound
The waves emerged, cresting white froth & shadow.

Stepping back from the edge, my hands were slick. I wiped
Them onto my clothes. My clothes became heavy.

I removed them. Now wetness poured forth from my navel.
All the coarse hairs of my body dripped at the tips.

The finer hairs exuded mist. Without tears, my eyes
Ran water, cold & saltless. I went to speak but found my mouth

Filled with a stream that rushed out as my lips spread open.
All my senses were given over. Through the undersides

Of the waves, the birds were a black erratic sun,
Turning smaller by distance, clearer as I drifted down.

And when I died, my life returned, steam burgeoning
From the kettle, a fly flirting with the day's first meal,

The vents sighing out the conditioned air onto my shoulders,
Over the backs of chairs, around the table's limbs.

A restoration, but still I am inconsolable, like a room
With its door kicked in, from which the thief has fled, & my face

Cracks with age, a riverbed broken with drought,
A floe shattered by the fist of spring, & I thirst for the stark

Torrent, gone forever, whose diamond-blood spills to stain
The rocks, the roots, the streets, the tongue, where I taste the source.

SOUL IS THE SELF REFUTING THE BODY

My wife in the dentist's chair, after hours.
A few nerves in her head pump their fists
At an obliterated heaven.

She's so filled with pain, I become jealous
That with her anything other than me
Can get this intimate.

Like someone's breaking a bottle against my face.

For a moment, her eyes are porcelain. She goes
Somewhere, her head nodding
With the slow grace of a sinking ship.

Those nerves—slight, a scrap.
Once removed, you could smear them from existence
Between your fingers,
Playing the world's smallest violin.

But right now they are in there, & my wife comes back
& achieves an expression that uncreates
The caves of Lascaux, the Dewey Decimal, the Magna Carta...

Latex gloves ply the necessary
Implements, working.
Best not to look, says the man
On fire to the man with the knife in his chest.

My wife in tears, my heart a perforated sack,
My veins a mess of cords, my brain
A weak battery animating a dumb machine.

It may be that we're just a spattering of savage atoms
& when the embers dim in each cell
We aren't even allotted the cold or blackness
Or the thought thereof.

So what. I hear that a god lacks nothing,
Which proves its uselessness.

I will speak against it. Speak this language
Black & blue, defy, lurk, squirm, spit ourselves into being,
Because we are found wanting, and only that which wants
Has breath, has need, has cause to complete the cicada's husk

Still clutching the outdoor sill
Near the window in a room where I watch her,
The terrifying fluorescents harmonic

Inside their fixtures,
Fears & devotions towering through us,
Somewhere, here. Changeless. Untouchable.

CONSTELLATION

Now & then I believe that nothing asks for us.
Stars leak out their diminutive light & would get on fine
If we didn't gaze up to give them compliment.
They flame & die, unaware of our affections,
Of how, above a city, obscured by our ambient electrics,
They are desire's nebula, or from a wide pasture speartips hurtling
Through the deep of time. To be & bear itself,
Unknowing, kept from care, this isn't pain for a star.
What do I want to say? The spheres & fires hang
Their magnitude beyond our horizon, & practice distance.
According to Zeno, if space is infinitely divided,
You & I are forever far enough away to wish upon.
Tonight, your fingers tracing figures across my thigh
Is the only paradox worth understanding.
Let it be true. In another sky, we are brightening
Our vastness, two restless points of navigation
Set into an image that shifts & wanders.

MAKING

Angel is a word
I no longer care for. So is
Fracture. Who doesn't

See, when he sees, the lines
All around him—the tops
Of pines needling

The distance, the
Many rivers, which are
One river— who really

Doesn't & hope it makes
A figure, indestructible, pure?
Who doesn't want also

To break the lines?
There's nothing for it.
With sorrow, you are

Building the trees,
The water, smashing them
Joyfully, putting

Them back together.

STEWART BEACH

A blue monolith on dense smoked glass—the sky & sea.
The pressure makes an edge so elegant
It can slit a person's throat.
This is a lamp, the toddler who has just dug out
A spark plug from the sand says.
Her father does something unmentionable
Inside the foyer of his skull
To the creature three towels over, tanning facedown
With her top undone.
A little grit falls from his wife's finger
Onto the bread as she makes the sandwiches.
An appetite, even the wind has one of those.
The wind with a thousand tongues but no stomach,
Unappeasable, stirring the shoreline's aromatics—
Fish-rot, oils, a deliquescence in the trash barrel,
Damp cloth. The water itself
A brute fragrance—half putrid, half mellow.
The umbrellas loll their shadows.
The girl hurries to the waves, yelling *Sewer Beach*
& pauses a few steps in. Behind her, the pavilion.
Its snack bar closed, the decking blanched,
A limp spray pushing away relics
Of the ocean's climate from the swimmer at a showerhead
Near the stairway. The father walks
Into the sea to join his daughter.
They move out further until the sand dips low.
There is an instant where the sea might pull
Her out for good, & she laughs at it.
The mother's arm sways overhead on the shore, calling.
Bright in the heat, the pavilion
Looks ancient & pathetic, an afterglow
That will not diminish, almost hovering.

AFFIRMING THE SELF

Some have a slow dance with death. In the cruel gymnasium
The bleachers retract to make room for the refreshments.
Shrimp curl around the lip of a cocktail platter.
The sauce cold & sweet & red.
A punch bowl tinkling with ice & a plastic ladle.

The song, sad but popular, music we grew up with, repeats
For the awkward couple, one partner wearing
A black corsage, the ubiquitous lover.
One all pimply & dreaming about getting laid.

Leave them there. For us
Death is a shifty confidant, the friend who has fallen
Out of touch, who has left you hurting,
Who is perhaps right now returning to sit beside you on the couch,
Unfold a secret, something personal, & make amends.

Until then, the crape myrtles are permitted to get loud each April,
Blaring their colors like a high school band.
The cars can peel out in empty lots
As glaciers sigh & collapse into the ocean.

Among the universe's clatter, you are allowed your insignificance,
Which lets a famous bronze boy standing over
The fountain's basin in Brussels,
Naked & weathered, pissing a cool stream in the face
Of eternity, stay somehow glorious.

Cut Lilies

My grandmother lay for eight
Days in her Manhattan apartment:

She yellowed the third-floor tenement walls
With mouthfuls of smoke,

Was a civilized racist, once sang
With Lena Horne, once lost my brother

& me at Penn Station
When we were small, shopped

Through curbside trash,
Cursed our mother, swam naked,

Used all the wisdom she had...
They sent my father word by mail

& he identified
The body from a photograph.

Air cools & passes around me
Like a strange silent crowd

In search of a city.
I seem to love her here

Ten states away
With the windows open,

The neighborhood
Doing nothing in particular,

While these faded blooms
Continue to cloud my sense

With beauty, enriching
The atmosphere of this living room,

As they have for days
& I've just only noticed.

EPISTEMOLOGY OF THE HAND

My hands are pockets, deepening, where the world
Drops in & through
                    The holes at the bottom.

In winter, I keep warm
                    Smearing together their emptiness.

In fall all the brittle leaves I have ever touched,
                              Books, coins, thorns, the length of hair
        Through which
                    I ran my fingers & the keys

To doors I've left open & forgotten.
                              I stretch my

Eye down into my little palm, &
                              My whole face vanishes

        Like a sparrow with one torn wing, disappearing
Into the black oval of a tree's hollow,

                    Wounded & secure.

LOVE SONG

For M

This morning I make-believed your death:
A policeman phoned *There's been an accident*
So that my daydream tears rushed out
With cinematic alacrity.

In the gusto of my imaginings
I no longer found candy wrappers
Crinkling near the bedside lamp, or fled
The television so that I could read

My Tennyson in peace—bachelorhood.
Unimpeded by love, all my long life
Roared POSSIBILITY, nights & days
Without the usual, without you...

But inside the great mechanism
Of dream, something snapped like a long clean wire,
& it was true, briefly there at twilight,
True you didn't lie beside me

Soft-snoring in your underwear, all signs
That you exist hauled off the planet.
I grew praise like a hidden wound, & turned,
& wished you back sleeping where you were,

You who had never left, the regular
Goddamned-beautiful you I held at dawn,
My hands vigilant, a wind swaying
The curtains at the opened window.

MATERNITY WARD

In the seventeenth hour of the twelve
Thousand two hundred & ninety-second day
Since my birth, I can reveal
Nothing more about the magnolia flower
Dolloped on the lawn underneath
This hospital window that you probably haven't
Already learned yourself.
The afternoon is a color that must be
What a mosquito sees from inside a piece of resin,
Its honeyed stasis. A nurse has checked the vitals,
& now there is only my wife slumbering
On a beige mechanical bed & our son
Resting on my forearm in a swaddle parading
A pattern of lions, his head in my palm.
The privacy curtains undertake a drunkenness,
Moving in a fabricated wind
Meant to keep us comfortable. The room is
Darkened, quiet except for the light passing
Through the panes & the weird wind & the constant numb
Groan of some obscure device &
I have just finished crying.
From exhaustion. From fear. From delight.
From staring out at the wad of thick cream petals
Too much a symbol of beauty to be good for anything real.
What other reasons are there.
My son's face is a gestural sketch,
The rendering of an amateur, clumsy but passionate.
He spits up vowels.
Yes, it enthralls, confounds.
But that's not what I'm saying.

There is the dagger I use to caress
& the dagger that is always the exact
Length between me & another person & the dagger
That stands openly in the doorway
Expecting my last arrival, & they are all the same.
But I'm not saying that either.
Only this. That once I was younger,
& after having left the car by the talus, we carried
A cooler & our sleeping bags well into the woods.
A copperhead lay in the leaves, & my friend
Severed it into a pair of twinging commas.
We came to the clearing where the earth goes
Sandy along the curve of the stream.
There was a moon in the sky, & in the face of
All the burdens that were to come upon us,
We drank with a sense of propriety.
By the fire, my other friend's eyes became silent
& looked down a caliginous path visible only to himself.
We slept on the ground, nothing above but the heavens,
If one can still call it that, abundant as ever
With luminaries we can't harness or devastate
Or disavow or glory in without a fool's aplomb.
Who knows why. I rose at twilight & my fingers
Skimmed dew from my cheek while the day broadened,
Each shutter opening in the great house
From room to room, taking its time.
The stream was performing a score it had begun
Long before the first spasm of chemicals
That constitutes my thinking, your thinking. Thought altogether.
And it played a derelict chord,
Within which I heard my own ugliness & arrogance,
& it was a comfort to have my failings intoned,
To be strange, still waking.

I never got over it. I am always a vagrant there listening
To the water, crushed into an oblivion,
Though I am other places as well.
I have just one mind, but I've got many hearts.
One gets divided into morsels to be gnashed
By men with commemorative pins in their lapels.
One is packaged in a kerchief & sent to the lady-in-waiting.
One has been left with no price marked on a shelf
At the local convenience store.
One was hooked up inside the governor's chest when
He wasn't looking & flinches at two hundred
Beats per second, though he can hardly tell it's there.
One sweats in a vitrine at the Museum of Natural Science.
One I've lost, but on nights
When I roll out the trash I reach
Into the neurotic calm of the boulevard
Where the streetlamps chalk the lanes & curbs,
& the homes are piles of obsidian,
& I've heard it cooing, *Aieoo heh. Wah. Gah goo ga.*

NOTES

The title **Of Bodies Changed** is from the opening line of Ovid's *Metamorphoses*, translated by A. D. Melville.

Naming was written on the occasion of the 2006 exhibition *Chance Encounters: The Formation of the de Menil's African Collection* at the Menil Collection, curated by Kristina Van Dyke.

The title **Storms Are Formed Behind the Storm We Feel** is from a line in Herman Melville's poem "Misgivings."

The quote within the first line of **Report** is from book XI of Plato's *Laws*, translated by A. E. Taylor.

The narrative of **Lines Toward an Illuminated Manuscript** was inspired by an anecdote relayed by Toni Nelson.

In **Stewart Beach**, the phrase "sewer beach" was supplied by Walker Hipps.

APPRECIATIONS

My ardent thanks to Craig Beaven, Brad Hipps, and Jim May—my friends, accomplices, and literary advisors. I'm also grateful for my teachers, most especially Bruce Bond, Mark Doty, Tony Hoagland, and Corey Marks. I thank my friends, past and present, at the University of Houston Creative Writing Program, many of whom helped in shaping the poems within this book. For the same, my gratitude to the Happy Criminals—C.B., Lauren Berry, Hayan Charara, Brandon Lamson, and Glenn Shaheen. For making my writing life possible during an important period, and that of so many others, my thanks to the people of Inprint and its terrific staff—Marilyn Jones, Kristi Beer, Krupa Parikh, Lee Herrick, and the incomparable Rich Levy. For being an exceptional group of people, my friends and colleagues at the Menil Collection, with special thanks to Toby Kamps. For their love and support, the Hyland, Rodrigues, and Murphey families. I owe Stanley Moss a debt for his guidance and belief in my work.

And for everything, always, Missy and Miles.